How t

Organized

Learn How to Declutter and Organize All Areas of Your Life So You Can Retake Control, Be Productive and Have a Clear Mind

Mitch Jensen

© **Copyright 2020 - All rights reserved.**

The content contained within this book may not be reproduced, duplicated or transmitted without direct written permission from the author or the publisher.

Under no circumstances will any blame or legal responsibility be held against the publisher or author for any damages, reparation, or monetary loss due to the information contained within this book. Either directly or indirectly.

Legal Notice:

This book is copyright protected. This book is only for personal use. You cannot amend, distribute, sell, use, quote or paraphrase any part, or the content within this book, without the consent of the author or publisher.

Disclaimer Notice:

Please note the information contained within this document is for educational and entertainment purposes only. All effort has been executed to present accurate, up to date and reliable, complete information. No warranties of any kind are declared or implied. Readers acknowledge that the author is not engaging in the rendering of legal, financial, medical or professional advice. The content within this book has been derived from various sources. Please consult a licensed professional before attempting any techniques outlined in this book.

By reading this document, the reader agrees that under no

circumstances is the author responsible for any losses, direct or indirect, which are incurred as a result of the use of information contained within this document, including, but not limited to, —errors, omissions, or inaccuracies.

Contents

Introduction 1
Chapter 1: Impact of Clutter 3
    What is Clutter? 4
    What Exactly Does Clutter Impact? 5
    What is Behind the Clutter? 7
Chapter 2: Minimizing the Clutter 11
    Why Cluttered Home is Problematic 11
    How Does a Cluttered Home Impact the Mind 13
    Areas to Cover 15
Chapter 3: How to Organize Your Home 17
    A Methodical Way 17
    Floors, Closets and Drawers 19
    Getting Assistance 24
    How to Organize a Home 25
Chapter 4: The Messy Work Environment is The Killer of Productivity .. 28
    Why is Lack of organization at Work an Issue? 28
    How to Improve Your Focus 30
    Virtual Clutter 30
Chapter 5: Making Your Office Organized-- A Guide 32
    How to Organize Your Desk 32
    Tackling Your Hard Disk Drive 33
    How to Organize Where You Work 34
Chapter 6: How Organized is Your Life? 37
    What is a Cluttered Life? 37

Why do our Lives End Up Being Disorganized? 39

The Issues With a Packed Life 42

Chapter 7: How to Organize Your Life 44

Dealing With Responsibilities and Dedications 44

How to Use Social Media Less 45

Reassessing Your Routine 47

Say No 48

Chapter 8: Does It Make Sense to Organize Relationships? 50

Do You Have Problematic Relationships? 51

What is a Harmful Relationship? 51

Classify Your Relationships 52

How to Cultivate Worthwhile Relationships 55

Chapter 9: Clearing Your Mind 58

The Indications of a Messy Mind 58

Why You Want an Organized Mind 59

Chapter 10: How to Have an Organized Life 62

Lists and Journals 63

Letting Go 64

Don't Multitask 67

Make Firm Decisions 68

Have Self-Respect 69

Conclusion 72

Thank you for buying this book and I hope that you will find it useful. If you will want to share your thoughts on this book, you can do so by leaving a review on the Amazon page, it helps me out a lot.

Introduction

Are you having a hard time concentrating on anything in your life? Feel nervous and worried? Is it tough to inspire yourself to get anything accomplished? The issue might lie in your chaotic mind.

Modern life is busier than ever before. The majority of us feel hurried from early morning to night. Handling household dedications, work responsibilities, personal problems and social life all take their toll. The large quantity of obligations and tasks that we need to fit into every day can appear mind-boggling. It is exactly this that triggers psychological clutter.

The bright side is that, even if you're discovering life difficult to manage at the moment, by putting some organizational strategies into practice, you can make a massive distinction in your physical and psychological wellness. You can reclaim your life, enhance your focus, minimize your diversions, and get rid of your stress points.

When you eradicate the psychological clutter, you'll discover that you'll get more accomplished and you'll feel a lot better in general. With better organization comes more precision and control, so you can see more plainly the path in which you're heading and focus on the things that are crucial to you.

Chapter 1: Impact of Clutter

Nowadays, we have actually all ended up being more accustomed to living with a great deal of things in our lives. Yet, when those things get out of control it can result in us feeling swamped, ending up being less efficient, having a hard time to focus, and being without inspiration. This is the "Clutter Effect."

Yet, lots of people have no idea simply how disorganized their lives have actually ended up being. They have actually ended up being so accustomed to shuffling the many aspects in it, from relationships and kids to buddies and careers, that they can't see the wood from the trees. Ultimately, however, the confusion is going to end up being so huge that they will not have the ability to work successfully at all. For that reason, understanding what clutter really is, how to recognize it and how to remove it lies at the heart of getting overall success and joy.

What is Clutter?

When you think of clutter, you most likely think of stacks of documents and magazines tossed over your counter tops and piles of scrap on the stairs waiting to be taken up. It holds true that this is clutter-- however, it's just the physical type. Your mind can end up being messy too.

Invasive thoughts, a continuous list of "must-dos", remorses of missed out on opportunities, incomplete work, and stresses over things that may never ever take place are all instances of psychological clutter that makes us feel out of control. The less arranged your mind ends up being, the less you feel able to handle the difficulties that life tosses your way.

There is a limitless cycle formed in between psychological and physical clutter. The more messy your mind, the more messy your house, work area, and life, generally, are going to end up being. On the other hand, if you're living and doing work in a messy environment, it's inescapable that your mind is going to end up being messy and chaotic too. The vicious cycle causes continuous issues as you do not have the capability to break the chain, do away with the mess and take your life back.

What Exactly Does Clutter Impact?

As we have actually currently mentioned, clutter impacts both your environment and your mental and emotional wellness. Both kinds of clutter can have a significant influence on numerous aspects of your life.

The initial apparent part that can feel the effect is your house. Mess can start to develop as duties get left negated. Quickly, a stack of magazines has actually grown on the coffee table, a stack of shoes is in the corner in the front porch, and clothing items are accumulated on the chairs. The more messy and untidy your house ends up being, the more difficult it is to get inspired to sort it out, and the more unfavorable the emotional and psychological effect becomes of residing in such an environment.

The 2nd essential part that is terribly impacted is the work environment. An absence of organization in the workplace causes all types of concerns. Low performance, a less than professional impression for customers or visitors, and bad spirits are simply a few of the issues that occur because of a messy workplace. Once again, once the workplace has actually ended up being messy, it ends up being harder to do something about it to arrange it. As the mess accumulates, the worse the associated issues end up being.

The 3rd part that feels the effect of mess are your private relationships. This is something that can frequently be neglected when thinking about the impact of a lack of organization on your life. An unpleasant house puts stress on your family life and can result in severe stress with your kids, partner or other loved ones.

A messy work environment can make working relationships with associates, supervisors or employees more difficult and can result in differences that trigger long-lasting issues in your profession. Not just that, however, mess in relationships can result in toxicity, additional tension and a lot more commitments that have to fit into your currently inundated schedule.

What is Behind the Clutter?

There are numerous reasons for clutter. Some are physical, and others are mental or psychological. Some are likewise a lot more apparent than others.

Possibly the most apparent reason for clutter are the excess physical belongings. The majority of us are guilty of collecting things since we can't bear to eliminate them, even if we do not truly require or desire them. There are presents that we have actually gotten for birthdays, keepsakes from holidays gone by.

Things have actually accumulated for many years that ought to truly have actually gone in the garbage and which have, inexplicably, been placed on a rack or in a drawer for later and stayed there. The problem with this kind of mess is that it develops gradually, so you do not actually understand just how much it has actually gotten out of hand up until one day you take a look around and see the level of the issue.

The 2nd reason behind clutter is having too many dedications in your schedule. We have actually currently pointed out how hectic modern-day lives have actually ended up being. Whereas in the past, lives were much easier-- individuals went to work, got home, hung around with their buddies or family, and after that, went to sleep all set to do all of it once again the next day.

Nowadays, there is a lot more to think about. Professions have, in most cases, ended up being substantially more high-pressured, with the expectations put on employees at all levels much higher than in the past. Domesticity is likewise more intricate than ever before, with lots of people having actually mixed or split families. Having a hard time fitting in contact with kids, handling stepchildren or needing to manage an ex-partner in addition to an existing one can all boost the pressures on daily living.

Then, obviously, there are all the other aspects that weigh on our minds. An unlimited stream of social networks and 24/7 access to the news can quickly result in us ending up being swamped with negative thoughts. On the other hand, we feel the pressure to maximize our minimal free time by caving into the needs of associates, buddies, and members of the family to go to various occasions and take part in different activities.

We additionally push ourselves to exercise, to enhance ourselves and to be the very best that we may be in every regard. It's no surprise that a lot of people have a hard time coping as we sink ever-deeper under a stack of dedications, responsibilities and demands.

Chapter 2: Minimizing the Clutter

Initially, let us have a look at the house. A messy house results in a messy mind. Then, we'll take a look at some mannere in which you can lower the mess so you can restore some necessary control over your life.

Why Cluttered Home is Problematic

Why do we wind up acquiring clutter in our houses? There are a number of explanations behind this. Let us take a look at a few of the most typical:

- You do not understand when it's time to do away with things-- in lots of homes, there is a great deal of confusion about when the time has actually come to sell, donate, shred or discard things when they're no longer required or utilized.

- You do not have a place to keep things appropriately, or you simply do not understand how to stash it.

- You have no organization regimen to follow in the house.

- You do not have enough storage area or solutions.

- You frequently purchase things that you do not utilize or require.

- You do not have the capability to let go of things, particularly those with some nostalgic worth

Much of us can associate with a minimum of one of the above. The secret is to determine which applies to you to ensure that you can then deal with them.

How Does a Cluttered Home Impact the Mind

Mess in the house winds up having an unfavorable effect on your body, mind, and your total health. There is a direct link in between high levels of tension and excess mess in the house, and this has actually been shown in a number of research studies over the past couple of years. Why is this the case?

The house is meant to be a sanctuary of calm-- a serene haven and a comfy area where you can relax. How can you do that if there is a lack of organization and mess all over? Mess in the house adversely affects your capability to concentrate and focus. There are diversions all over and this triggers your psychological faculties to end up being worn down. Disappointment is then the inevitable result which induces tension to develop. When you can't concentrate correctly, your capability to solve problems and be innovative is likewise hindered.

Tests have actually demonstrated that individuals who have actually boosted clutter in the house likewise have greater cortisol levels in their bodies. Cortisol is a stress hormonal agent that activates a flight or fight reaction. When levels of this hormonal agent are elevated, we can not really unwind or relax efficiently, and we're continuously in a state of high alert. On the other hand, those whose houses are tidier and more arranged have less stressed out and better lives.

One additional issue that clutter can trigger in regards to psychological health is the sensation of guilt that can accumulate in time. Understanding that you ought to be keeping your house pristine, however, not appearing able to discover the time or inspiration to do the job can increase anxiety and stress levels. That makes it even more difficult to unwind or enjoy yourself throughout your possible downtime. You're continuously thinking of all the many chores and tasks that are unfinished and that still have to be accomplished.

Areas to Cover

The typical house has numerous parts where clutter can start to gather and accumulate. Nevertheless, there are 4 essential parts that you ought to take a look at initially when preparing to get arranged and to reclaim control of your life.

Initially-- have a look at your floorings. Do you have stacks of things in the corner of the space? Do you have home furnishings that merely use up area in your house? Choose how you can utilize the space better to ensure that you can move more quickly in between spaces and delight in optimal openness throughout.

Second of all-- have a look at your drawers. Are they filled with scrap? Have they been arranged and cleared just recently? Are there things in there that ought to truly have gone in the garbage years ago? Even if there's no scrap in there, have they been arranged and cleaned?

Third-- have a look at your closets. Do you truly use all those clothing items? Are all those shoes truly needed? Could you discover brand-new storage options to make the most of the area in your closet?

Furthermore-- have a look at your racks. While these might be the last part that you think about arranging, it could be the location in your house where most clutter appears. How frequently have you placed a toy, a book or a pen on a rack and believed you would move it quickly, however, then never ever got around to it? Do you routinely clean up the CDs, books or DVDs in your systems? It's time to give them a once over to do away with any things that do not belong on a rack.

Chapter 3: How to Organize Your Home

Are you all set to arrange your house to recover your life, yet, aren't sure where to begin? Then here is a total guide to assist you in starting the undertaking.

A Methodical Way

To be effective in arranging your house, the secret is to take a methodical way. Decluttering your house is a significant undertaking, so tackling it in phases is an excellent idea. You might choose to start with a single space and completely sort it out prior to carrying on to the following space.

Or you might select to take on a single zone within one space, for instance, the cabinets, prior to proceeding to the rest. In either case, taking a methodical way lets you see the outcomes, albeit little ones, from every undertaking and assists to boost your inspiration to continue.

There's no requirement for any expensive devices or tools when it pertains to decluttering your house. All you require are 5 baskets or bins. You ought to tag them as follows:

- Place away-- the things you place in here are going to be those that have actually, in some way, wandered off from their initial storage area. They have to be returned in the proper area.

- Recycle-- this is for things that need recycling such as glass, paper and plastic.

- Repair -- this container ought to be utilized for things that require fixing, mending or cleaning.

- Garbage-- if the thing is no longer required by any family member, and it would be no good to recycle or donate, toss it in this bin to place into the home garbage.

- Donate-- if you do not desire a thing any longer, however, a charity or another individual might desire it, you can place it in this basket.

Floors, Closets and Drawers

As soon as you have actually got your baskets prepped and your method set out, you can start dealing with the drawers, floors, cabinets and closets. It makes good sense to start in a single area, work through it entirely, and after that, move onto the following one.

It might be an excellent idea to start with your restroom, considering that the mess here is most likely to be reasonably low. Start with the medication cabinet-- dispose of any out-of-date items, medications or makeup, and right away, place all things to keep back in the cabinet.

Carry onto the drawers. Take all the things out, choose what has to be kept and what has to be tossed out, and then place the things you wish to keep back in the drawers. Repeat with the shower and tub and other things from beneath your sink. If any things stay that are not garbage, sort them rapidly into the 5 baskets so you can handle them later on.

The bedroom is a larger job. It makes good sense to start with your nightstand. Get rid of anything that does not belong and arrange it into a suitable basket. If there are any things you do not utilize, such as an empty tissue box, a damaged battery charger or a pen that does not work, do away with them.

Next, proceed to the chests, dressers and bureaus. If any clothes are scattered around, place them into the laundry in case they require cleaning, or into the put-away bin if it is to be tucked into a drawer or hung up. Clear your office, cabinets and drawers and place any things that are still in fine shape, yet, that you no longer wear into the donation basket. Place away all of the other clothes nicely.

Regardless of how enticed you might be to put things back into drawers or cabinets, stay clear of that temptation. Place them into the put-away basket and handle them later on. Recycle or discard any things that have not been utilized for 6 months or more.

The closet is the next huge task. The simplest method to tackle it is to arrange clothes by type. Go through each classification and sort your things into 5 stacks. One is going to be to keep and return in the closet. One is going to be for things that are in the improper location. One is going to be for dirty laundry. One is going to be for things to be dry cleaned up or fixed, and one is going to be for things to be donated.

Carrying on to the entrance, you'll discover that even the tiniest area is going to have some mess to be handled. In case you have a side table, desk or a console, deal with that initially. Get rid of all things in the drawers and choose whether to keep them or throw them. In case you have a hall closet, declutter it similarly to your bed room closets.

The kitchen area is a significant area to address, and it can additionally be the toughest to maintain clutter-free in the long-term considering that a lot of activities occur there, from eating and cooking to interacting socially. You'll, for that reason, have a great deal of things in it. You can decide to either go through each zone one by one or concentrate on a single group of things prior to proceeding to the following.

Totally empty your selected area. Examine each thing. Discard anything that is unneeded, and then place the other things back tidily. The pantry and upper cabinets are an excellent location to start prior to carrying on to the drawers, lower cabinets and under-sink location. Last of all, concentrate on the counter tops and attempt to move as much as feasible into storage areas.

The last location to deal with is the living-room. This is a specifically challenging area to attend to given that it sees a great deal of usage and might not have storage. To start, pick where you're going to keep all your typically utilized things such as your magazines, books and push-button controls. Then start decluttering your side tables, bookcases and console prior to proceeding to your coffee table and entertainment center. Place any books away. If there is any documentation to handle, place it to one side, and fold any blankets.

Inspect your electronic things and ditch any that do not work. Store any video gaming devices, controllers and battery chargers in a practical yet concealed area. Last but not least, if there are any toys lying around, examine them for damage and examine if they still work. If your children do not have fun with it any longer, recycle it. Place any other things away tidily.

Getting Assistance

When you're attempting to arrange a whole home, it could be a significant undertaking, particularly if you're living in a big home. If this relates to you, it's time to acquire some assistance in the form of your buddies or loved ones.

Get the children to assist with decluttering their own spaces and putting away their own things. Make certain they understand where essential things are going to now be kept away so they understand where to place them back after usage.

If you have no buddies or loved ones to assist you, you might have the ability to discover a cleaning company that is going to provide you some help with the undertaking.

How to Organize a Home

Want a couple of more best suggestions to assist you to arrange your house and your mind? Here are a few of the very best:

1. Start in one location. Choose which area is your priority and begin there. Concentrate on it up until it's totally organized prior to proceeding.

2. Enable sufficient time. Have sensible expectations of the length of time it'll take you to completely rearrange your house and schedule a couple of hours daily to the task at hand.

3. Take a stock. After any undesirable things are eliminated, check what stays and choose if it remains in the incorrect or right location. Anything that would be much better off elsewhere, move it there.

4. Look for squandered area. Can you see any extra space that might be used? Areas over doors, beneath beds or beneath sinks might be ignored, yet, might hold important storage room.

5. Think vertically. This is particularly essential if you reside in a little house. Optimize your storage by shelving right up to your ceiling.

6. Split up spaces. If you include more racks to a single rack or utilize baskets or stacking containers, you can split up vertical areas, make the most of storage and keep all the things looking nice.

7. Think about wheeled storage systems that could be moved around or kept in a closet when not being utilized.

8. Keep in mind the keywords-- flexibility, visibility and accessibility. Select clear containers or ones that you can tag quickly to

spare time. Make sure that you have actually put the most often utilized things in an area that is simple to gain access to and pick an adaptable storage system that could be reconfigured and recycled.

Chapter 4: The Messy Work Environment is The Killer of Productivity

Now that we have actually taken a look at attending to the lack of organization in the house, it's time to move onto the work environment. Here, we take a look at why mess in the workplace triggers many problems.

Why is Lack of organization at Work an Issue?

When you remain in a messy work environment, there are hosts of problems that start to emerge. Some have a private impact on you, others impact your coworkers, and some are going to even affect the success of the business adversely.

When the work environment is jumbled, chaotic and untidy, anxiety and stress can start to develop among staff members. Not knowing where to locate anything can cause differences, arguments and an unfavorable environment in the workplace along with high tension levels.

Without any effective system in place and mess getting in the way, it naturally follows that the whole group ends up being less efficient. Important time is squandered on looking for lost things or attempting to reorganize things that are getting in the way. Workers are additionally less inspired in an chaotic, untidy environment, so efficiency levels drop all around.

Let's include into the mix the truth that an untidy workplace produces a bad impression for anybody going to the properties. Whether those visitors are clients, customers or business contacts, when they see a messy work environment, they instantly get the incorrect impression about the business and believe that it's a less than professional company. This additionally adversely influences the success of the business.

How to Improve Your Focus

The initial step to ending up being more concentrated at work is to get rid of any physical mess. Desktops, cabinets, drawers and other surface areas in the workstation ought to all be offered an overhaul and any undesirable things ought to be recycled, discarded or returned where they belong, tidily and nicely.

When your immediate workplace is tidy, arranged and clean, it ends up being simpler to focus on the job at hand. You can rapidly see the things, documents and files that you require so no time at all is going to be lost. You'll additionally feel a lot less nervous and stressed out when things are where they should be.

Virtual Clutter

Remember that lack of organization in the work environment does not end at your desk surface area. The virtual mess is another major issue that can start to pervade through your mind and trigger minimized efficiency, overall tension and poor motivation.

Your e-mail folders and hard disk drive could be a source of anxiety and stress for you if they aren't kept in some type of reasonable order. The virtual mess can create just as many issues as physical lack of organization, or perhaps even more. If you can't discover the crucial file that you have to send out to an associate, or you're trawling through unlimited e-mails searching for an immediate message that you have actually lost yet have to reply to rapidly, your tension levels can skyrocket.

Tackling this virtual mess is a crucial part of decluttering your office. It is going to make a remarkably huge distinction to your psychological wellness.

Chapter 5: Making Your Office Organized-- A Guide

If you're prepared to start making your work environment more arranged, yet, aren't sure where to begin, here is some guidance.

How to Organize Your Desk

The initial step to tackling your desk organization is to declutter any visual diversions. Art work done by your children, numerous images of your last getaway, inspirational phrases-- all of these could be messing up your efficiency and stopping you from concentrating at work.

Have a look at the things that are on your desk. Any documents or files that ought to be placed away in the right areas ought to be placed away now. If there are pens lying around in front of you, check to see if they function, and if they do not, toss them in the garbage.

Do you see old papers, articles or marketing material? If they're unnecessary, recycle them. Look once again at any old files or binders to examine the contents. If the documents and info within are old or will not ever be required once again, do away with them. Be callous.

Tackling Your Hard Disk Drive

A virtual mess can be just as damaging for your psychological wellness and your performance as a physical mess, so start by restructuring the computer system desktop. If files have actually been saved there for many years or icons are jumbling your entire screen, you'll have a hard time to recognize the ones you require rapidly when you require them most. Erase any unnecessary icons or files and clean up the others so you can have an efficient screen.

Tackle your e-mail inboxes too. It's all too simple to permit your e-mails to get out of control, particularly if you get hundreds daily. Nevertheless, setting some time aside to organize your folders and to erase the garbage is going to assist to make things workable once again. If you identify any neglected messages, respond to them and submit them nicely in a folder where you know you can locate them once again.

As soon as your inbox is neat, it is necessary to remain on top of the job. Reserve time every day to look at e-mails and manage them properly. Make it your objective to have no inbox messages prior to going to sleep.

How to Organize Where You Work

Do you require more ideas to effectively arrange your work area? Here are a couple of pieces of professional suggestions that are going to help you a great deal.

- Chuck the scrap-- have you utilized a thing in the work environment just recently? Are you reasonably going to utilize it once again? Just as you would in your home, produce different stacks to be handled later on. 3 stacks ought to do here-- a store stack, a garbage stack and a to-do stack.

- Produce a reliable storage system. As long as it makes good sense to you, it is going to do the job.

- Tackle the to-do stack. Make folders for each customer or task you're dealing with. As quickly as the task is done, go through the folder and toss out any unimportant files inside. Then, store away the folder in a proper place.

- Preserve a clear desk. As soon as your desk surface area shows up, reserve time weekly to remain top of this. The one-touch guideline can aid with this. Generally, as quickly as a paper touches your desk, handle it quickly. Bin it, do something about it, or submit it. This applies to messages and e-mails.

- Utilize technology in the very best manner to spare yourself time and effort. Keep an online organizer to integrate your calendar, to-do list and address book in one place.

Chapter 6: How Organized is Your Life?

Now that we have actually dealt with the mess that develops in the house and the work environment to trigger lack of organization, mayhem and bad psychological health, it's time to look more carefully at your life. It's highly likely that your life is additionally struggling with some serious lack of organization if you feel as though you're missing control.

What is a Cluttered Life?

As we have actually currently stated previously in this book, we tend to think about mess as a physical thing, nevertheless all-too-often it could be emotional or psychological too. When your life is jumbled, all of that mess and lack of organization is unnoticeable-- it's within your head. Yet, that does not make it any less difficult to handle. As a matter of fact, it makes it a lot more difficult to handle.

What does a chaotic life appear like? How do you understand if you have one? There are numerous indications that you can watch out for to inform you that you're struggling with this issue.

To start with, you have a schedule that is encumbered with activities. You appear to be hectic for each single hour of the day, without any time to invest in yourself. You feel as though you're continuously at the beck and call of other individuals, whether those individuals are buddies or members of the family, and you have a hard time to fit all of your dedications, commitments and activities into your currently stretched way of life.

You feel as though you have positively no free time when you can relax and enjoy yourself. Or, when you do manage to get a couple of minutes for yourself, you feel guilty that you're not dealing with the many other things that you have actually lined up prepared to go.

You feel under increasing pressure to be a much better individual, to enhance yourself. You feel guilty when you do not have the time to prepare a fancy vegan meal from scratch or fall short to get to the fitness center once again today or didn't manage to get to your foreign language class so you might expand your horizons.

If you can connect to any of this, you have a chaotic life that needs to have to be de-cluttered quickly.

Why do our Lives End Up Being Disorganized?

There are a number of reasons that your life might have ended up being chaotic. Not all are going to apply to everybody, however, if you're experiencing the things described above, you'll likely acknowledge a few of them.

- You're overlooking your own standard requirements and are, for that reason, making bad choices. This can result in tension, anxiety and stress and compulsive thoughts that stop you from concentrating on more vital parts of your life.

- You have FOMO or fear of missing out. This is a really 21st-century issue, and an extremely typical one. It's something that moves you to register to the fitness center when you merely do not have time. You take an additional class even when you're having a problem with the ones you have. You scroll through Facebook for another hour instead of going to sleep. Or, you head out for a night at a club with buddies despite the fact that you understand you need to get up for work early the following morning. While FOMO originates from a location of wishing to delight in a much better life, it can wind up making your life even worse by including more tension, anxiety and stress and diversions.

- You have a hard time letting go. This might apply to both psychological and physical luggage. Even if something is triggering discomfort, or is making you dissatisfied, you still have a hard time to release it and this triggers you to dwell on it, repeatedly.

- You have not discovered what is enough. You still feel that you, in some way, need to be much better, more ideal, to get more things so you can be worthwhile of approval, love and appreciation. You have not understood the principle that good suffices and this leads you to stress over things in your head that make you unfocused, dissatisfied and non-productive.

- You can't say no. Some individuals simply do not feel able to place their foot down, even when they actually do not wish to do something. They're too anxious about the response they'll get or about distressing somebody and losing their relationship if they defend what they require and desire.

- You feel obliged to do things, even when they aren't your obligation. You have not comprehended the concept that delegation is a good idea, and you fret that you'll lose your significance if you permit somebody else to handle a task that has constantly been yours.

The Issues With a Packed Life

When your life is overwhelming, a host of issues can follow. The poor organization of an over-packed schedule leads you to struggle with bad psychological health. You end up being significantly stressed and nervous about how you're going to fit all the things into your congested day, week or month.

You additionally wind up without any quality time on your own-- something that everybody requires every now and then to charge their batteries. When every second of the day is accounted for, you simply do not have sufficient time to unwind, relax and release all the aggravations that you have actually come across.

Falling under the bed at the end of a tough and long day is going to typically cause poor quality sleep as you have a hard time to process all of the pressures and tensions you have actually gone through. This only serves to make it much harder to discover the inspiration and energy to manage the difficulties that life tosses at you.

When your life is disordered, you'll additionally discover that your relationships end up being significantly stretched. Ultimately, you'll end up being more annoyed, more upset and most likely to snap at your member of the family and buddies. This is going to increase stress in the house and make life a lot harder.

Chapter 7: How to Organize Your Life

Are you prepared to take control of your life again and find out how to arrange it so you can take pleasure in much better psychological wellness? Then keep reading for a couple of best ideas.

Dealing With Responsibilities and Dedications

The primary step is to take a look at your different dedications and commitments. Do you truly require all of them in your life? Could you stop with some activities to provide yourself more time to loosen up or spend it with those who truly matter?

It's time to remove anything that you can live without or that makes you anything less than delighted. If it isn't needed and you do not like it, and it's feasible to ditch it.

Next, be selective when handling any brand-new activities. Prior to accepting anything or jumping right into something brand-new, put in the time to consider it. Do you actually wish to do this brand-new activity? Is it going to include something favorable to your life? Or is it going to be a drain on your psychological resources? Decide based upon your answers.

How to Use Social Media Less

Social networks are among the greatest reasons for FOMO. It stands to reason that we take a look at other individuals' profiles and typically feel envious of the lives that other individuals appear to be living. Nevertheless, it is essential to keep in mind that most of the times, folks show the image of their lives that they desire others to see instead of illustrating the genuine fact of their circumstances. A family can seem excellent on a Facebook profile, however, the members might all be suffering on the within, without those scrolling past acknowledging it.

Never ever compare your interior to other individuals' exterior.

If you're discovering that social platforms are triggering you to have a hard time psychologically, or you're discovering that you're investing increasingly more time scrolling through pages instead of proceeding with your life, it's time to minimize your social network use.

How do you start with this? You may discover that an easy location to start is merely to sign out of your profiles when you have actually ended your session. If you need to go through the rigmarole of signing in every time you wish to look at your alerts, you'll quickly start to decrease your use.

If this does not work for you, you need to attempt leaving your phone in another space or in an unattainable area for part of the day, and never ever keeping it by the bed during the night. This is going to assist you to restrict the quantity of time you spend on social networks.

Reassessing Your Routine

Are your regimens triggering you psychological pressure? Then it's time to give them an overhaul. It could be all too appealing to remain stuck in a rut due to the fact that change is frightening, however, that's seldom an excellent thing to do when you have actually lost control over your life.

Have a look at how you spend every day. Which parts of the day are inducing you to have a hard time? How could you move them around to make life simpler or less difficult?

For instance, if you have actually arranged a workout at the fitness center prior to going to the workplace, however, you're having a hard time rising since you're going to be so tired that it will be tough to concentrate at work for the remainder of the day due to the fact that you do not have energy, it's time to take a look at how you can make changes. Think about moving the gym to after work, and even to your lunch hour, and take some additional time in bed so you could be well-rested and boost your efficiency at work.

Say No

Among the very best things that you may do to arrange your life better is to simply say no. Do not be scared of harming other individuals or of losing their love or relationship. No one who cares for you is going to think any less of you if you back out of a dedication that you do not have time for, or if you decline to go to an occasion or take part in an activity due to the fact that you merely can't fit it into your life.

Saying no could be really challenging, specifically if you have actually never ever truly done it previously. Nevertheless, as soon as you begin practicing, you'll discover it really liberating. You are never ever going to have to accept an invite that you do not wish to accept once again. You'll never ever have to go to an occasion that you dread or take part in a lengthy activity even if another person desires you to do so.

In some cases, it's okay to put yourself first, and when you're attempting to reclaim control of your life and enhance your psychological wellness, it's completely appropriate to refuse politely.

Chapter 8: Does It Make Sense to Organize Relationships?

All too frequently, we wind up in relationships that induce us more issues than joy. Many people are going to acknowledge the circumstance of a so-called buddy who just appears to be thinking about their own issues-- who constantly appears to be asking you for aid, however, then never ever appears to be around when you require their help in return.

Lots of people are incredibly knowledgeable about having a buddy who just appears to come around when they desire something, or when they wish to whimper and grumble. If you have a buddy who brings you down instead of lifting you up, it's possible that you might gain from some relationship organization.

Do You Have Problematic Relationships?

Messy relationships are one last element of a messy life that can cause a chaotic mind and bad psychological wellness. If you continuously feel as if you're needing to put somebody else first without that individual having an identical approach to you, you're most likely in a hazardous relationship.

It's human nature to attempt to latch onto the relationships that we have actually formed, however, often, those relationships just aren't worth conserving. When a relationship brings you suffering and not joy, it's time to think about letting it go so as to declutter your life and improve your psychological health.

What is a Harmful Relationship?

How do you acknowledge if you remain in a hazardous relationship? It could be tough to identify a poisonous buddy. It's feasible that they were once a best friend who was beneficial and kind towards you previously. It could be hard to see how a relationship like that can weaken in time, therefore, you may ignore the telltale indications of toxicity for a long period of time.

Frequently, jealousy is the origin of a hazardous relationship. Possibly you got a better job, began a family, or dropped weight. Your buddy might find it difficult to handle their own sensations of inadequacy and might start to put you down, treat you severely or something similar.

Classify Your Relationships

Classifying your relationships is going to bring you more exactness in your life. You can separate your buddies into 2 groups-- radiators or drains.

Does your buddy bring coziness into your life and make you feel great and happy about yourself? If they do, that's fantastic. They're a radiator. Nevertheless, if they empty all the love, positivity, joy and strength from your life, it's a hazardous relationship and your so-called buddy is a drain.

When you understand which of your buddies are drains, you can act. You might have the ability to cut your hazardous buddy entirely out of your life. If they are somebody you just saw irregularly anyhow, you can simply stop texting, calling and setting up meet-ups. You can erase them from your social networks. Yes, you'll most likely feel guilty and uncomfortable, however, it's for your own good.

Meanwhile, if it's somebody that you're still visiting frequently, you might have to use another strategy. You can hide them on social networks so you aren't subjected to their negativity daily. Unfollowing somebody indicates that they will not notice that you can't see their posts, however, you'll be devoid of the toxicity and back in control.

Because you can't alter a hazardous buddy's character, you'll have to alter how you respond to them. Do not permit them to make you feel little or bad about yourself. Rather, say to yourself that your buddy has the issue and that there's absolutely nothing amiss with you. It could take time, however, in time, you are going to acquire back control and power.

If it's feasible, attempt to decrease the quantity of time you devote with your hazardous buddy. If you remain in the identical location at the identical time, attempt to create a buffer with other individuals. However, if this person continuously puts you down in front of others, simply leave the group when that person approaches or respond with a non-aggressive, calm action that turns any snide remarks back on the provider.

We naturally wish to get approval and appreciation from individuals in our lives, however, if you have a hazardous buddy, you can wind up feeling even worse about yourself. When you have actually been injured in this way, attempt noting all the important things you feel excellent about yourself for. Jot them down and check out the list whenever you feel like this.

How to Cultivate Worthwhile Relationships

When you have actually recognized which of your buddies are radiators, you have to feed those favorable relationships to ensure that they grow. Attempt to devote as much time as feasible around individuals that make you feel great about yourself.

How can you promote those favorable relationships? Here are some professional recommendations to point you in the appropriate way:

- Take some time to listen. Listening skills are crucial when it concerns increasing your buddy's self-confidence and self-regard. You have to listen to what your buddy has to state, and you likewise have to work to comprehend what they are conveying to you to ensure that your interactions could be as effective as possible.

- Be Present. Even if you're physically with somebody, that does not indicate that you're actually there. If you're dwelling on another thing rather than truly listening to what your buddy is informing you about, or if your mind is roaming rather than truly taking notice of what they have to say, you aren't promoting a favorable relationship. The connection you make with your buddies is the base of that relationship's success, so you have to commit sufficient time, energy and effort into developing and establishing the relationship to ensure that it can flourish and grow.

- Offer feedback and take it in return. This is an essential part of a strong relationship.

- Be someone who can be relied upon. It takes nerve to trust somebody. Nevertheless, it is essential to keep in mind that the more you rely on your buddy, the more open you are to positivity.

Chapter 9: Clearing Your Mind

The secret to happiness is to unclog your mind of all the clutter and mess that is hampering and obstructing your psychological wellness. However, how do you tackle clearing your mind? How do you even know that your mind is jumbled to begin with?

The Indications of a Messy Mind

How do you understand if your mind is jumbled? There are a couple of telltale indications to watch out for:

- Stress and anxiety

- Tension

- Poor focus

- Absence of motivation

- Low performance

- Sleeping disorders

If you're experiencing any or all of these signs regularly, you're probably experiencing a messy mind.

Why You Want an Organized Mind

The actions detailed previously within this book about removing the clutter from your life, relationships, work environment and house can all assist you to have a well-organized mind. So, what are those advantages of a well-organized mind?

Maybe the greatest benefit is the sense of wellness and calm that you'll experience as soon as all of the mayhem is out of your head. As soon as you have actually eliminated all the clutter and mess, you'll have the ability to acquire a restored concentration on the important things that actually matter. You'll have the ability to increase your efficiency by having the ability to focus on the job at hand with no undesirable diversions because of the thoughts and ideas churning around in your head.

You'll additionally end up being more definitive. As soon as your mind is clearer, you'll find out how to get more control over the decisions that you make in every part of your life, and you'll find out how to make those decisions sensibly and clearly. You'll quickly have the ability to see the path forward plainly and will have the ability to move forward with no interruptions or issues.

Your tension is going to be considerably minimized too as soon as you have actually removed all of the unneeded garbage from your head. When you're no longer completely in fight or flight mode, you'll be much better able to unwind, relax and take time out for self-care. This is going to permit you to take pleasure in much better wellness, both physically and mentally.

Lastly, the most crucial advantage of all is that you are going to attain more joy. When you have control over your life, you can feel positivity and inner peace. Consequently, when you feel positive and happy, you remain in an excellent location to get even more out of life, feeding a favorable feedback loop that is going to make your everyday life a far better one.

Chapter 10: How to Have an Organized Life

So, now that you comprehend all of the advantages of a put-together mind. You have to understand how to get to that point.

We have actually currently taken a look at the practical actions that you can take in the house, at work and in your private life to eliminate the mess and mayhem. This can make life better and easier, however, how can you take reasonable actions to arrange your mind?

Here are a couple of things to get you going.

Lists and Journals

Many individuals discover that making lists or beginning a journal is a great way to clear their minds. It is going to eliminate all the mess that stops them from moving on in their lives.

You might discover that you're not able to concentrate on the activities that you have to perform since they appear to be running over and over in your head. Making up a list of all the chores and tasks that you have to do is going to assist in setting those invasive thoughts totally free. Having a list of all the things you have to get done is going to assist you to see at a glimpse all that needs to be completed by the end of the week, day or month. When you can tick every one off, you are going to experience a terrific sense of wellness at work well done.

Journaling is another helpful method. It could be utilized to excellent impact to clear your mind and eliminate the mess that stops you from progressing with your life.

You might be feeling nervous, depressed or stressed out about circumstances in your life. Keeping notes in a journal is going to assist to bring a bit of clearness to the circumstance, and allow you to discover how to forward. It is going to additionally assist you to let go of the stress that develops when you're not able to express yourself and release the sensations that are triggering your torment.

Journaling additionally assists you to identify patterns in your life. It assists you to recognize exactly what makes you feel unpleasant, stressed out, nervous or upset. You can act to stay clear of those triggers or resolve them in a healthy manner the next time those scenarios appear.

Letting Go

It could be difficult to discover how to let go considering that a lot of us are raised in an environment where we grasp onto things, whether those are belongings, relationships or feelings.

Everybody is going to go through times in their lives when they feel dissatisfied, annoyed or upset. This is entirely ordinary and is something that can not be stayed clear of. The secret to conquering those emotions, however, hinges on how you handle them. Do you dwell on them, and ponder over them consistently? Or do you discover a method to let them go?

Psychological turmoil and mess can take place if you do not release the unfavorable feelings and emotions that you're grasping onto for dear life. The more time you devote concentrating on them, the less time and energy you have for the good feelings that you require to get the most out of life.

While all of this makes good sense, it could be more difficult than you imagined to let go of the negativity. So, here are a couple of ideas to assist you:

- Face the discomfort. If you're feeling stressed or nervous, your kneejerk response is going to be to shield yourself and conceal from the psychological turmoil. Nevertheless, you have to go through this negativeness to start the procedure of healing. If you postpone the procedure, you'll never ever have the ability to totally conquer what you're feeling.

- Do not lie to yourself. Recognize every part of the unfavorable feelings you're experiencing. Do not attempt to tell yourself that things aren't as bad as they might be. Rather, recognize it, acknowledge it, and after that, accept it.

- Keep in mind that absolutely nothing is going to last permanently. Unfavorable feelings are more powerful than good ones, however, you need to keep in mind that, regardless of how bad it feels, they will not last permanently.

- Self-reflect. Do not get caught in a damaging descending spiral. Review what's taken place and figure out how you can prevent coming down into a pit where more bad things are going to undoubtedly be.

- Do not fear the future. Although you have unfavorable feelings now, the future is colorful and you can rise and accept it just after you let these damaging emotions go.

Don't Multitask

We're all attempting to handle more than at any other time in history, so it isn't too unusual that all of us attempt to multitask. Yet, this isn't as handy as you may envision.

Multitasking is going to make you less, not more, efficient. Proof has actually revealed that if you move in between activities, you can squander as much as 40% of efficient time. While you believe that you're attaining more, the odds are that you aren't. If you put all of your concentration on one job, it is going to be finished more effectively and likewise better. Multitasking has an unfavorable effect on the quality of the output you create.

It's even been demonstrated that multitasking has an adverse impact on the way your brain functions, slowing it down and making it less effective. That indicates you have to remove unneeded interruptions that are triggering your psychological mess and limit your focus to the job at hand.

Make Firm Decisions

When you have the ability to decide and adhere to it, you can actually weed out the turmoil that fills your head when you have not planned a particular strategy.

While it might sound easy to decide, the truth isn't constantly that simple. A number of us fluctuate in between possibilities and have a hard time coming down on one side or the other when there are 2 various possibilities.

The trick to definitive and efficient decision making is to concentrate on what's truly essential and to remember that satisfaction is probably not going to be instant. You need to be self-disciplined as soon as you have actually devoted to a strategy and not be lured to fall at the initial obstacle. If you do not stick to the choice you have actually made, you'll never ever have the ability to attain a clear mind and reclaim control of your life.

Have Self-Respect

If you're to really arrange your mind and discover inner peace, you'll have to learn to begin being kind to yourself. While the majority of us know that compassion brings much better quality to your life, a lot of us still fall short to provide ourselves the self-care that makes us better and more positive.

However, what does being kind to yourself really suggest? Basically, you need to find out how to nourish yourself. After all, you can't depend on compassion being demonstrated to you by strangers, however, you can constantly demonstrate it to yourself.

Being kind to yourself suggests caring for your own psychological and physical wellness. It indicates having actually disciplined health routines and living a well-balanced way of life. This can be found in the shape of getting a sufficient quantity of quality sleep, exercising to reinforce your muscles, keeping your heart healthy and assisting you to remain versatile, and drinking a lot of water. It suggests going to the medical professional if you experience a health issue and embracing healthy coping systems to get you through the tensions and difficulties of daily life.

Keep in mind, as well, that being kind to yourself is a continuous procedure. It does not imply taking a number of days to support yourself if you're feeling particularly distressed or low. It implies taking routine time every day and week to take care of your wellness. Do not wait up until you're sick to take care of yourself. Do not wait till you're tired prior to relaxing. Prevention is much better than treatment, so make certain you embrace an upkeep self-care routine.

Conclusion

Regardless of how hard we attempt to keep a clear head, it's unavoidable that we'll all experience psychological clutter every now and then. Nevertheless, the secret to joy and reclaiming control of your life is to discover efficient methods to become clear-headed and to eliminate all that turmoil in your mind to discover a favorable path forward.

Clutter can be found in numerous shapes, from physical mess in the work environment or home, to psychological luggage that you carry with you anywhere you go. Mess can even be available in the shape of poisonous relationships. Somebody who is expected to take care of you might just trigger you more distress and suffering rather than positivity and joy.

In this book, we have actually taken a look at the many manners in which you can take actions to arrange your life. We have actually taken a look at how you can start to declutter your house to ensure that you can reside in an arranged, favorable and inviting environment. We have actually additionally taken a look at how you start to arrange your office, both in regards to physical things and virtual clutter.

We have even taken a look at how you can take action to bring more structure into your life. You can provide your schedule an overhaul. Find out how to say no to activities and occasions that you just can't fit into your schedule. Determine the important things that actually matter prior to including brand-new dedications into your life.

We have actually addressed how you can restrict your social network use to assist you to end up being more efficient and less caught up in the psychological tension of comparing your life to that of other individuals. We have also analyzed how you can identify a poisonous relationship and how you can then set about handling it while additionally working to nurture and support the favorable relationships in your life.

Lastly, we have actually thought about how you can clear the mess in your head. Utilize methods such as creating lists and journaling to get the feelings and sensations out of your head and onto the page. Letting things go, staying clear of multitasking and being as kind as you can to yourself are all crucial elements in reclaiming control of your life. It is going to enable you to carry on to a favorable, orderly future.

I hope that you enjoyed reading through this book and that you have found it useful. If you want to share your thoughts on this book, you can do so by leaving a review on the Amazon page. Have a great rest of the day.

Printed in Great Britain
by Amazon